The Accelerator Survival Guide

The Accelerator Survival Guide

How to lead, design and execute great programs

Sean Percival

Percival Publishing

CONTENTS

Table of Contents

About the Author

Sean Percival is an American entrepreneur, investor, and author from California. He has invested in 100+ startups and founded several of his own. He has been a startup accelerator Program Director at over 10 programs throughout the world.

As a former Investment Partner and Program Director for 500 Startups, one of the most well-acclaimed startup accelerators in the world, Sean has a unique depth of experience in accelerator management. During his time at 500 Startups, he ran several programs including the 500 Startups flagship program in Silicon Valley, in addition to programs in other parts of the world. These programs touched on all stages of startups from the very early stage pre-accelerator type programs all the way to later stage Series A growth programs. During his time there, Sean helped to create and implement several new accelerator frameworks and processes that are still used to this very day at 500 Startups.

Additionally, Sean has helped establish or worked with several other accelerator programs such as the Katapult Accelerator and various industry-specific programs. Through these programs, Sean has been lucky to work directly with hundreds of startups from all over the world. This has given him unique insights into the good, bad, and ugly of running accelerator programs. He's taken this wealth of experience and packaged it up here as a guide for accelerator program directors and staff members.

About this Book

This guide is a collection of experiences, frameworks and startup accelerator best practices. It's the ideal starting point for Program Directors but any member of an accelerator's staff can find value within its pages. Learn how to maximize your program and avoid the major pitfalls with this true survival guide.

After reading this book you'll understand the techniques and mindset of successful Silicon Valley accelerator programs. Discover how to build your accelerator team, recruit your startups, run a high impact program, and pull off a successful Demo Day.

You are reading version 1.0 of this book. In true startup fashion, I'm releasing this book in an early and imperfect state. In the words of LinkedIn founder Reid Hoffman, "If you're not embarrassed by the first version of your product, you've launched too late".

Additional and further expanded versions will be released throughout 2020. For Kindle readers, you'll receive the new editions automatically and at no additional charge. Those who purchase the paperback edition can also receive the Kindle edition for free.

Be sure to visit http://accelerator.guide for templates, updates, and even more survival tools.

Introduction

Welcome to The Startup Accelerator Survival Guide.

Before we get started, let's talk a little about what exactly a startup accelerator is. Popularized in Silicon Valley, but replicated throughout the world, these are short-term programs focused on, you guessed it, accelerating a startup. This can mean different things but typically these programs pay some attention to helping a company scale its business metrics and secure funding after completing the program. This is not to be confused with an incubator, which is typically a longer-term program and an initiative with different goals. For example, a university will often have an incubator to develop student ideas or build technology that needs a lot more time and funding.

Although these two concepts are often interchanged I like to think about startup accelerators as educational, content-heavy, and hands-on programs occurring over 1-3 months, whereas incubators are much longer-term (sometimes taking place over years) and less hands-on. Let's also not forget about startup labs, startup studios, corporate innovation programs, venture builders and so on. What can I say? We like to make up a lot of names in the tech industry. There's nothing wrong with these other company builder models, but for the purpose of this book, we'll be sticking primarily to the 'traditional' startup accelerator way of doing things.

Many of the ways startup accelerators work today can be traced back to the most well-known program, Y Combinator. To use techie developer speak, they are the 'master branch' and the rest of us are just a 'fork' of that branch. The humble origins of Y Combinator also reveal much about how accelerators took their current form, mimicking a summer school-like educational style format. The first batch was even named the *Summer Founders Program* and targeted students directly by offering the program (and investment) as a much better alternative to a boring summer job.

"Some friends and I have started Y Combinator, a new venture firm that specializes in funding very early stage startups. Our first project is the Summer Founders Program, an experimental replacement for the conventional summer job.

The SFP is like a summer job, except that instead of salary we give you seed funding to start your own company with your friends. If that sounds more exciting than spending the summer working in a cube farm, I encourage you to apply."

- *Paul Graham, Y Combinator Co-Founder March 2005*
  And with that announcement, Y Combinator was born. Paul Graham would later admit that they didn't expect their first batch

of companies to do very well. It was more for them to learn how to become good investors. Although there was one company in that first batch that has done fairly well. That company being Reddit, which has become one of the most visited websites in the world. However, through the course of that first batch, the Y Combinator founders learned something perhaps more important than how to become a good investor. They began to see the benefits of investing and working with multiple companies simultaneously, something that had never really been done before. *"Initially we didn't have what turned out to be the most important idea: funding startups synchronously, instead of asynchronously as it had always been done before. Or rather we had the idea, but we didn't realize its significance."*
• *Paul Graham Y Combinator Co-Founder March 2012*

Sometimes called a batch, or a cohort, this is the real essence of a startup accelerator program: **A shared learning environment and the sense of community that it creates**. It's actually a very special feeling and perhaps the most important key to the success of your own program. If you can capture just an ounce of the excitement, pressure, and hard work found in programs like Y Combinator, then you're probably running a decent program already.

That all being said, don't feel you need to emulate Y Combinator or other leading programs to be successful. Learn from their experience but make sure to make your program your own. Don't try to create 'the Y Combinator of xyz', instead create your own vision, investment thesis, and unique approach. This book will hopefully help guide you.

GETTING STARTED

Building a team

Just like building a startup itself, the team is everything when it comes to running a successful startup accelerator. There's a lot of moving pieces to these programs so you're going to need a few extra hands to manage them. Unfortunately, there is not a super deep talent pool when it comes to people with accelerator management experience. It's still a somewhat new industry and only lately have we seen exponential growth in the number of programs taking place around the world. So that means you might have to get started with some junior or less experienced team members. Sounds not too dissimilar from a startup, doesn't it? While this book is primarily geared towards accelerator managers, feel free to share it with any member of your staff.

As you build your team there are a few core roles that every program should have in order to support the needs of all the moving parts of a successful program. Oh and not to mention to avoid burning out in the process. Let's take a look at each of them:

Managing Director/Investment Partner

At the highest level, the CEO or Managing Partner is typically the most experienced team member. They have both prior investment and operational experience and are able to handle any challenge that comes up. Former venture capitalists and even former founders can make great candidates for this role. If they can lead sessions that's also great, although from my experience they are more often behind the scenes, ensuring the program has the capital and other resources needed to function properly.

The Teacher

They are the most comfortable in front of a group or on stage. They are a generalist who can speak on a wide variety of topics such as marketing, sales, fundraising, and pitch prep. They are 'the professor' on staff leading the bulk of the educational content. In most cases, they are a former founder and have often gone through accelerator programs themselves. If you have run several batches already, it's helpful to look at your alumni and see if anyone stands out as a potential candidate for this role.

Program Manager/Director

The program manager is the glue of any good program. They manage the program and also manage the daily calendar before, during, and after the program. This puts them in charge of communicating activities, in addition to making all activities run smoothly. In many cases, they will also be the ones responsible for managing the mentor network, guest lecturers, and myriad other things. Regardless of their gender, they are often considered to be the 'mother' of the program. They have all the answers as the role relates to program logistics. They also typically manage the operations folk and interns as well.

Operations Manager

With attention to detail and the ability to manage both people and spaces, the operations manager ensures everything runs smoothly. This includes the operations of the accelerator program office space and also event management. They may also be in charge of coordination between mentors, partners, and speakers. They work hand in hand with the Program Manager/Director on just about everything program-related. They are the right-hand man/woman to that role and support them very closely.

Investment/Legal Associate

With each accelerator program, there is much to manage with regard to investment documents and legal paper wrangling, so it's best to have a junior to mid-level associate solely focused on this. Their primary responsibility is to complete the investments in every company and manage the longer-term legal requests that come up. They can also support the due diligence process of screening the companies in a program. Completing startup investments is a complicated and grueling process, especially when dealing with large batch sizes of 10 or more companies. This role helps to drive that process so the other team members can focus on program execution.

Entrepreneur in Residence (EIR)

These former founders can be thought of like super mentors. The best profile is a founder who has recently sold or left their startup. They are in between startups or recently had a successful exit. So at the moment, they are discovering what they'll be working on next. A great outlet for them is often an accelerator as it allows them to work with many ideas and business models at a time. In other words, they need inspiration and you (hopefully) have gathered several inspiring ideas into a single venue for them. As a bonus, you get really experienced founders working closely with your batch. When possible it's helpful to have several EIRs involved in each program. This is often a part-time role and may or may not be compensated.

The Interns

Similar to the benefits an EIR might receive working in your program same goes for people at the beginning of their startup journey. Although they may have more energy than experience, startup newbies can still be very helpful in the form of program interns. They can help with odds and ends and even directly support your batch companies. You can usually find the best intern candidates from the entrepreneurial programs at your local college. If you pitch it to them as an opportunity to turbocharge their startup experience, and maybe even to get a job with one of the companies, you'll have no shortage of signups. It's also recommended to compensate them for their time. From my experience, I've found that interns who are not compensated are less engaged and in many cases disappear altogether. If you value their time and allow them to continue you may also find that today's intern can become tomorrow's program manager if given the chance.

Investment Structure

Many accelerator programs offer investment alongside the program they run. The dirty secret of the accelerator business is that running programs is actually not very profitable. Quite the opposite actually! Most programs are run at a loss with the returns being wholly dependent on the investments in startups themselves. If you're launching an accelerator program to build a big profitable business you're not likely to find it.

Whether your program includes investment is up to you and depends on your own situation and business goals. There are many programs out there, especially corporate ones, that for example don't invest for equity in the companies they work with. One reason for this is that it's actually rather challenging to manage the sheer volume of investments an accelerator can make during its lifetime. Not to mention the longer-term legal maintenance needs. If your program does not have a venture fund attached to it, or if your backing is corporate it might not make sense to make investments with each program. Additionally, some programs are run as a public service (government-backed) or for corporate branding and marketing. They are not returns-driven and there ain't nothing wrong with that.

That being said, the quality of startups you can attract will dramatically increase when an investment is available. It is, of course, a big decision for a startup to spend several months with you, so for the startups, the investment helps to cover costs incurred and time lost working on other things. The general thinking is that you'll also work harder for them in trying to increase their company's value. As we say in our industry, it's all about having skin in the game.

There are many great books written on the subject of startup funding. If this is all new to you I would recommend '*Venture Deals*' by Brad Feld and '*Angel*' by Jason Calacanis to get started. In this book, '*The Accelerator Startup Guide*' we won't be going into such depth of investment structure and terms. However, I'll share a few things I've learned over the years with programs that included a financial investment made into the companies.

What are the terms?

As you interview startups and build your pipeline this question will come up again and again. Startups who are talking to accelerators are particularly sensitive about this topic, specifically with what valuation a program invests at. Of course, if a startup was killing it and growing rapidly they would be getting lots of great offers from venture funds. However, if they're talking to you this is likely not the case. Still, they are programmed to try to get as much money for as little equity as possible. Herein lies the problem.

Startup accelerators don't invest at typical startup terms and there's a reason for that. An angel investor may write a check but they are usually not very active in the company. An accelerator program, on the other hand, will spend weeks and months hands-on with a company, in addition to longer-term alumni support. An accelerator's contribution is different from an angel's, and in some cases, their contribution is even more hands-on than a venture fund. Accelerators are also typically investing very early. This means that they are accepting much higher risk and therefore warrant a lower valuation. Much to the dismay of the young founders, this is sometimes hard for them to understand.

Sample Program Investment Terms

Program	Investment Amount	Equity
Y Combinator	$150K	7%
500 Startups	$150K	6%
Techstars	$120K	6%

As we can see in the table above, most of the well-known programs are investing at a roughly $2M valuation. For the markets in which YC, 500 and Techstars operate (like Silicon Valley), this is actually considered a really good deal for a good startup with traction. For comparison, a seed round for a similar company in Silicon Valley might value the startup at more like $4M-$5M, so the accelerator is getting a significant discount here. As every startup ecosystem and region is different in terms of valuation, you can use as a general rule that an accelerator program should be entering a company at about 50% of the valuation a local venture fund would invest at. Your ability to convince a startup you're worth such a deal will be critical to closing the best companies for your program.

As part of that convincing, you're going to run into a few roadblocks. First, for the founders, you want to show them that doing your program is a path to a *more* successful fundraise. Along with that, you'll help them attract better investors and get them the valuation they believe they are worth. It also helps if you can get them to understand that fundraising is a difficult and nebulous process with no guarantees. However, with your program, you can take something very murky and misunderstood and provide some clear direction. I've used the below image in welcome materials for several programs and feel it encapsulates this all very well.

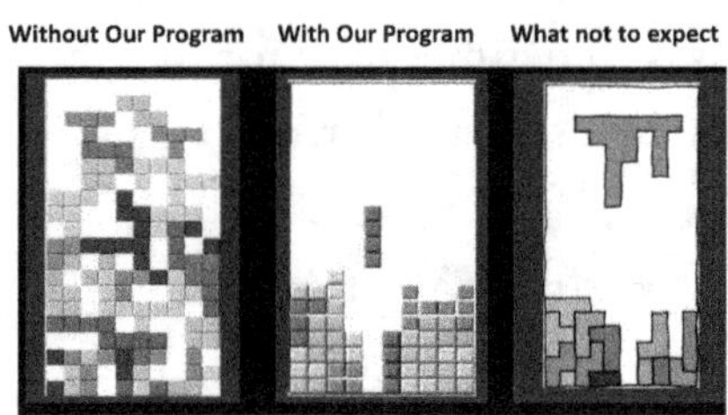

Another challenge you might face with regard to investment terms is getting buy-in from the startup's previous investors, board members, and advisors. I have in several cases been able to convince the founder to accept a program's terms, only to have a board member try to completely shut it down. Your best bet in this scenario is to talk directly to the concerned party and continue to sell the value offered by your program, explaining how the company will have a greater chance for success by attending your program. Sometimes this works but other times these parties are an unmovable object and unwilling to consider it. In that case, I go back to the founder and simply ask them, "Do you run your company or does someone else?", hoping to inspire some boldness in them to push the deal through. From my qualitative experience, early startups that have already ceded control to their boards are doomed to fail anyway, so perhaps you're saving yourself some trouble by having them opt-out.

Program Fees

There's one part of accelerator investment terms that's a bit controversial and that is charging startups a program fee for attending. Y

Combinator does not do it, and they go as far as to publicly call it "bad behavior". 500 Startups, on the other hand, have always charged a program fee and defended its use. Often the fee is deducted at the time of wiring the money. Effectively allowing the program to buy more equity for less. Here's how 500 Startups explains it in their FAQ:

"Yes – We charge $37,500 per company to participate, but these fees can be deducted from our investment amount so you don't have to pay out of pocket. As mentioned above, our gross investment is $150,000. Once program fees are deducted, you would receive $112,500. These program fees help to cover basic costs of running the Seed Program, paying outside speakers and should be viewed like tuition."

I've worked in programs that do both and I don't have any strong convictions against charging a fee. In fact, I think for new programs where your operation budget might be limited it's your best way to get a financial boost. I've worked on several programs that just would not be able to operate without the program fee. Just be mindful that some founders will push back on this or decline a deal due to the program fee. I recommend a ratio of roughly 3:1 in terms of investment size to the program fee. Anything more and you're perhaps being a bit too greedy and may scare away good startups.

Mentor Networks

As smart as you might be, you probably don't have all the answers between yourself and the accelerator staff. Enter mentors. These are experts in their various fields on the founder, investor, or corporate side of things. Almost every accelerator program has some form of a mentor network. Those that do typically enjoy overselling just how amazing that network truly is. The truth is that mentor networks are supplemental to your own staff and experience because at the end of the day, the more experience you have in-house and make available for your founder daily, the better.

Mentor networks can, however, be a powerful deal flow recruiting tool. Founders like to look at your web page and see lots of smiling faces from authorities in their respective spaces. That's because early-stage startups are eager to expand their networks but that can take a long time to develop. So they view accelerators and investors as shortcuts in this area. Just be honest with founders and yourself about their involvement in the program. I've found that it's better to have a bespoke approach with each startup you work with when it comes to mentors, their expertise, their involvement, dedicated time, etc. Match them up with a few of the right mentors instead of a large list of people that may or may not be relevant to their company. The stronger the match, the more valuable the interactions will be. In some cases, I also ask the founders to make a wish list of people they want to meet. That might be a specific person or just anyone in their industry.

As an accelerator manager, your main job is to deal with people. Mentors are the external rockstars you bring in to help the companies understand the lay of the land and prep them for when they graduate from your program. I've worked with a lot of them, and at the risk of generalizing, let's take a closer look at each type.

The All-Star:

Let's start with the best mentor you can possibly get on board: The all-star successful and well-known founder or business leader. They have proven they can build a big business and successfully exit it. In true 'pay it forward' style they now dedicate a fair amount of time to helping the next generation of founders. Due to their success, they are often cash-rich but time-poor, so you're typically lucky to get them to come into your program just once. They'll do a talk, usually in fireside chat format, and perhaps meet a few companies. Be respectful of their time and make sure they have a smooth experience so you can get them to come back again.

The Mentor Prostitute:

Let's swing the pendulum all the way now and talk about one of the worst mentors you can get: The mentor prostitute. They are mentors in no less than 20 other programs and proudly display that fact on their LinkedIn, website, resume and occasionally shout it from street corners. They have more advice to give than they have the experience to match, but that doesn't stop them from sharing it. They email you constantly, trying to become a mentor in your program. This is typically a red flag. The best mentors you'll have to recruit in, not the other way around.

The Investor Mentor:

Smart investors will actually be very open to mentoring in your program. They need a way to expand deal flow and you can really get to know a company by watching them for 3 months in an accelerator program. There is a very, very small chance they'll invest. But either way, it's a net positive for both parties. Given their experience, and as high-frequency meeting people, they are also the best candidate for setting up office hours sessions with batch companies. For even more value, ask your investor mentors if they'll do mock investor pitch sessions with your companies to better prepare them for the real-world investor meetings.

The Growth Hacker:

Since most startups in an accelerator program are looking to learn how to grow faster, these are great people and you need to have them in your mentor network. Ideally, you'll have growth mentors who are focused on online marketing (paid ads, searches, social media), and others who are more focused on the sales team and process development. Since this type of person typically also has a full-time job or works for an agency you can sometimes recruit them by allowing them to sell their services to companies in the batch.

The Intangible Mentor:

Building a startup is not just about the things you can touch like investment or growth hacks. It's also about the softer things such as people management, building confidence, and perhaps most important not burning out as a founder. To address these areas you also need mentors who are perhaps far removed from the world of startups. One example might include an expert on improv comedy to help founders speak more naturally. Or an expert of sleep health and nutrition for example to help founders live better lives and run at peak performance.

Sponsors and Corporate Partners

In general, startup accelerator programs have extremely tight operating budgets. After all, a program's goal is typically not to make money from running the program itself, but from the increased value of the participating companies. When you start tossing in costs like accelerator staff, event space to run your program, and travel, things can quickly add up. While it is certainly possible to run programs on a shoestring budget, a little extra operating cash can have a big impact. This is where sponsors and corporate partners come into play.

Speaking candidly, this is a bit of an oil and water scenario. You're trying to build and support small early-stage companies. Yet you have to do some pandering to these big slow-moving corporations who might consider sponsoring your program. But here's the thing! They also need you! They need you both for marketing themselves to the startup community and in some cases selling their services directly to startups. It's a mostly symbiotic relationship and something you'll have to manage as a program director.

First, it's good to know that almost no-one is going to want to sponsor your very first program. That's because there are many accelerators programs out there, with new ones popping up all the time. So the parties most likely to sponsor a program are probably already involved with one, or several programs. Additionally, as a new program, you don't have much track record to show. Sponsors often like to see operations running for a few batches, and the beginning of an alumni network. When starting out it's recommended to go for quick wins with smaller corporations, saving the really big fish for when you're more established. That might also mean much smaller sponsorships but it's a starting point and a chance to build a larger relationship. In terms of the price range, many of my newly established programs had sponsors only offering $2500-$5000. We took the money, and it allowed us to get to know the corporations and prove our value. Landing a really big corporate partner for your program can be a multi-year effort. But don't get discouraged, if you build a solid program and manage to run several cohorts, partners will start knocking on your door. Many established accelerator programs now command large sponsor levels as high as $500K annually and more.

When it comes down to the different types of partners there's really only two. Let's take a look at each of them:

Industry Partner

If your accelerator program is hyper-specific to a certain industry or technology, this will likely be your main sponsor. They are often a long-established leader in their respective industry. For example, if you're building a program focused on maritime and ocean startups you would be targeting every large shipping company out there. If you were doing a FinTech accelerator you would be in discussions with banks and financial players. Your best bet with this type is to engage with industry powerhouses who are not already involved in another program. An effective pitch here is to show them a path to learning a lot more about new technology, trends in their industry, and getting access to talented founders they may want to hire or acquire at a later time.

Service Providers

Here's a rather large category of potential sponsors for a program. This includes the likes of Amazon, Price Waterhouse Cooper, law firms, and so on. For them, their main goal in sponsoring a program is to sell their own services to the startups, at least the ones that get funding and can afford them. They may also do the sponsorship for some branding into the startup ecosystem as well.

In terms of how you structure the sponsorship, most programs offer some type of '*Gold, Silver, Bronze*' approach, or other multi-level offerings. How you structure these levels is really up to you. The industry focus and the tenure of your program will also be a factor in determining what you can ask of your sponsors. I would, however, recommend trying to land one large or a marquee sponsor, and getting them to sign up for an annual commitment with you. This may take some time and much effort, but in the end it'll be much easier for you to focus on keeping one large sponsor happy, instead of many, many smaller ones.

Sample Sponsor - Levels and Offerings
Gold

- Logo featured first and most prominently on the website
- Sponsor's name featured in the accelerator program brand name (Powered by *Your Corporate Name*)
- Host (1) sponsored session/workshop during the program
- (5) Social media shoutouts during the program (Tweets and Facebook posts thanking you for your support)
- (10) Tickets to Demo Day
- A booth at Demo Day to showcase your brand or product(s)
- Your logo featured at Demo Day (large) with rollups

Silver

- Logo featured on the website
- (2) Social media shoutouts during the program (Tweets and Facebook posts thanking you for your support)
- Your staff can attend (2) accelerator program workshops or sessions of interest
- (5) Tickets to Demo Day
- Your logo featured at Demo Day (small)

Bronze
- Logo featured on the website
- (1) Social media shoutouts during the program (Tweets and Facebook posts thanking you for your support)
- (2) Tickets to Demo Day

There's also another type of startup accelerator sponsorship in the form of in-kind services. In the business, we sometimes call these perks. While these don't usually put money in your operating budget, they do generate a lot of value for the startups in your programs. More specifically these are free credits and services from companies that startups typically need. An example of this is Amazon Web Services (AWS) cloud computing credits. They can also include other things such as lawyer hours, free software, or access to premium paid products at a discounted rate. Companies are smart to offer these cheap/free credits as a way to create lock-in with the startups in your program. They know once a startup has built on its services or platform it's hard for them to move even if/when they scale up. It's a sneaky but effective approach and as a program director, you'll want to forge relationships with many of these providers.

With the in-kind sponsors, there is one industry that is perhaps the most active with accelerator programs. That would be the cloud computing platforms. More specifically, the ones from Amazon Web Services, Microsoft Azure and Google Cloud. It makes sense - almost all startups need these cloud services and all these tech giants are eager to gain more market dominance. For the time being Amazon is the leader and one of the most active sponsors of accelerator programs. You can find them offering $50,000 or more in free cloud credits to programs throughout the world. From experience, I can tell you they are a great partner. Also from experience, I can tell you, much like Amazon as a whole, they are extremely data-driven. To keep them as a happy and active sponsor it's important to show them that a large portion of your startups both activate and use the free credits offered.

DEAL FLOW

Sourcing and closing high-quality deal flow is key to long term success with your accelerator program. Today, thanks to an explosion of accelerators around the world, the landscape is more competitive than ever. So in addition to the proper management of your deal flow pipeline, you'll need to work extra hard to attract the best companies.

For new accelerators launching their inaugural batch, this is going to be especially challenging. Without a track record to show and being an unknown brand, you'll need to work double-time to fill the first batch. That means doing a lot of outbound outreach to get meetings with companies that match your profile.

As a catch-22, the best companies will think they do not need an accelerator program. That's because they are already growing and typically overconfident about their prospects for raising additional funding. They will tell you things like, "Oh, we're way past the accelerator stage" and "we plan to close big funding next month". Neither of these things is usually true but we can't fault the founders for their optimism. I have found the best way to convince companies like these is to show them a path where doing your program will allow them to raise more capital and at a higher valuation. But first, let's learn how we make contact or get them to apply in the first place.

Getting Applications

This is actually one aspect of running an accelerator program that I personally really enjoy, which is probably due to my background as a marketing executive. I simply approach getting applications the same way a marketer would think about lead generation: It's all about a large and well-qualified top-of-funnel.

Let's look at a program with a batch size of 10 companies. To run a decent pipeline you could need as many as 1000 applications. The acceptance rates in these cases (as it is with leading programs like Y Combinator) is just 1%. For reference, the acceptance rate at Harvard is around 5%. For early and first batch programs you will probably not match these numbers and in fact have significantly fewer applications, but these are the benchmarks you should be aiming for. If you manage to get a few hundred applications your first time you are doing pretty good.

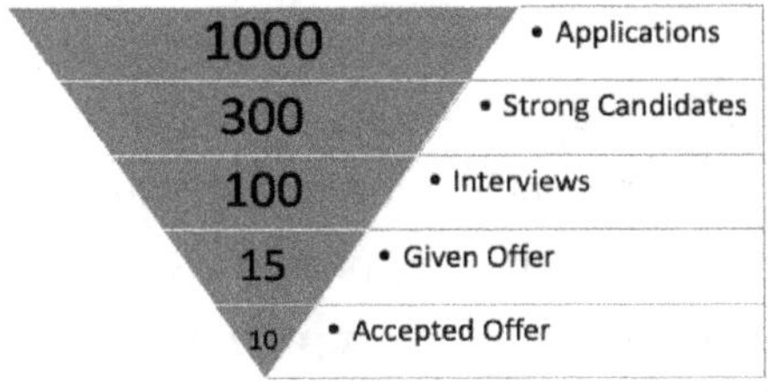

Getting Started and Application Marketing Channels

There are many channels in which you can find startups. Each program will typically need to market themselves in several different channels. This is especially true for your first few batches before you start to get some word of mouth marketing from previous attendees.

When it comes to capturing your inbound applications you'll typically want this to take place on your own website. While there are many services and startup portals that will gather applications for you, I've found in the end this is something you want to control 100%. Additionally, some of these accelerator application portals require you to exclusively use them to accept all applications. I would avoid this as it limits your ability to use another platform and ultimately retain control of the valuable data you collect.

While I'm not able to give you an exhaustive breakdown of how to capture and manage your application data here, I'll give you some friendly marketer advice. The dataset you're building with your program gets more and more valuable over time. It's also some of the only unique intellectual property (IP) you build with such programs. So treat your data well and start with a good Contact Relationship Management (CRM) software setup from the get-go. If everything you do with application data is in a big messy Excel sheet, you're doing it wrong.

The Application

Most accelerators use a similar application format which includes some 20+ questions for the founder(s). These questions can in many cases feel a bit overwhelming. But here's the kicker, this is by design. If accelerator application forms were too simple then programs would receive a lot of unqualified applications. By requiring so much information it serves to filter out some extent of the 'wantrepreneurs'(although don't worry, you'll still get lots of applications from them!).

The bar for getting into accelerator programs has risen over the years, so if a startup can't answer basic questions around their business they're probably not a good candidate. This all being said it's something to think about as you build your application form. The more information you request, the fewer applications you'll likely receive. Be careful about putting too much friction in the process. For example, in my programs, I've never required the founders to record a video introduction of themselves. My concern is that there are likely some very brilliant founders who are far too shy to record themselves. I'd rather have a larger top-of-funnel and do my own filtering of the applications.

The Basics	
Basic Contact Info	Email, Phone and so on
Company Name	Company name, and sometimes it helps to get the legal entity name as well for background research
Website	If a company does not have a website, this is a good sign they are too early for this stage.
Company Domicile	Find out where the company is incorporated to ensure it's a match for investment mandate or focus.

Date of Company Founding	Most accelerators work with companies that are 1-3 years old. Although there are always some 'late bloomers'.
Founder Name(s)	Get the founder(s) names. It's not important to know every team member but you should get an idea of how many founders are involved. Most programs look for 2 or more.
Founders LinkedIn	For your due diligence, it's nice to have direct links to LinkedIn for each founder. Browse these to look for the previous experience of the core team members.
The Pitch	
Company elevator pitch	Try to get them to give you a very quick pitch of what the startup does. When possible limit this field to less than 100 words. It's actually a big challenge for startups to do this well!
What problem are you solving?	Often for startups the problem they're targeting is more important than the solution itself. Is the market big enough? Are they solving a real pain point?
How does your product work?	Get some understanding of the solution itself and see if the founder can clearly articulate the value it provides.

Latest Investor Deck	Getting a copy of the latest investor deck can quickly tell you the stage and level of sophistication of the team. Any team without one is probably at too early a stage for most programs.
Traction and Funding	
What's the current traction of your main KPI?	Often this is revenue, but it can be other metrics as well. Look for how the founder articulates this number, is it a clear and meaningful way to measure traction?
Have you raised previous funding for this business?	Yes/No answer to help you filter the stage of each company. Companies who have not raised funding are not always a bad match, but they may be too early for some programs.
How much funding have you raised?	To understand previous capital into the company. Most companies that are an ideal match have raised some capital from angels. This can be a good external validator of the team and business model.
What was the valuation of the last investment round?	To better understand what the market has previously valued the company at. Although the range in valuation can be extreme, ranging from $500K all the way to $5M+.

You can add further fields to your application form if your program requires more information to help guide the decision-making process. Other things to ask include:

- **How many team members are full time?** To help to gauge the team's commitment to the business. A company where most founders are not full time is a signal they may not be ready for acceleration.
- **What do you hope to get out of the program?** To better understand the team's motivations and ensure your program's curriculum is a match.
- **How did you hear about the program?** To see if they were referred by alumni or found it through another channel. This also helps to inform which marketing channels are working with regard to attracting applications.

Applications Marketing Channels

As you begin to accept applications, start to build up the acquisition channels you can use for each program. While most of the highest quality deal flow comes from your own network there are a few channels that can also support your top-of-funnel. Let's take a look at a few of them:

Angellist (angel.co)

The de facto startup directory (at least when it comes to American startups) is a good place to list your program and scout for companies. They also offer an application tool that in some cases can bring in interesting leads.

F5S (f5s.com)

Another massive startup directory that is used globally. While most of the deal flow is very early stage here, there's a lot to choose from. They also run an accelerator application tool, although to get much marketing support from them you need to make it the default and exclusive way to apply to your program.

Facebook Groups (facebook.com)

One of the most powerful channels for getting exposure to your program is Facebook groups. Specifically, early-stage startup groups focused on a certain region or type of technology. Simply search away and you're bound to find several that match your profile. Post in these groups that you're taking applications in the least spammy way possible.

Other accelerators

Because of the sheer number of programs running these days, there are likely to be programs similar to yours. Or perhaps even slightly earlier-stage, making your program a good next step. Look at their websites and alumni companies and do direct outreach to startups of interest. It's also a good idea to build relationships with other accelerator managers. That way you can share deal flow when companies in your respective pipelines are better matches for each other's programs.

Remarketing/Retargeting (adroll.com)

For any program, it's a good idea to run retargeting advertising to all visitors who visit your site. In many cases, startups will take some convincing to fill in your application form. Or they'll just plain forget. Using these ads is an easy way to bring them back to complete the application. There are many ways to do retargeting but I personally recommend the service AdRoll.

So for early programs, you'll be doing a majority of outbound outreach to find your companies.

Over time and after completing successful batches you'll find that your inbound starts to gradually improve. In this business, word of mouth is everything. So don't underestimate how important it is to have a happy founder graduating your programs.

SURVIVAL PRO TIP

Founders are notorious procrastinators. They will often wait until the last minute, just as applications are closing, before submitting theirs. Don't be nervous if your applications are off to a slow start and save most of the promotion for your final week. It can help to include language like "Apply Today! We review applications as we receive them." on your application form.

Outreach and Scouting

For those early or inaugural programs, you'll be needing to do a lot of outreach to build deal flow. Being the new kids on the block in a crowded area means you have to work a bit harder. Still, even mature programs do a fair amount of outbound to land great startups. This reminds me of an experience I've had in my own outbound sourcing.

We were doing a lot of outreach while setting up a new program in Europe. During this time, a theme emerged where many of the companies we sourced had already been in contact with another program. It kept happening over and over, even when we found under-the-radar startups, or companies in not so typical geographies. This other program was Angelpad in the States, and the outreach was conducted personally by none other than the program's Managing Partner, Thomas Korte. Although Angelpad is perhaps a program that is not so well known, they have managed to recruit some amazing startups such as Postmates (which has surpassed $2B in valuation). It seems a solid ability to outreach to undiscovered companies is one of the keys to such success.

Scouting Outreach Template

Here's a sample template you can use as part of your outreach efforts. Make it unique to your program and even though it's a template, the more tailored the better.

Hello!

I came across <STARTUP NAME> while researching <YOUR INDUSTRY OR REGIONAL FOCUS>. What you are working on is really interesting and I would love to learn more.

I'm <YOUR NAME> and right now I'm recruiting for the <YOUR ACCELERATOR> program taking place in <YOUR LOCATION> on <YOUR START DATE>. Our program is focused on startups working in the areas of <YOUR FOCUS>. Additionally, we have experts and partners (<PARTNER 1>, <PARTNER 2> and more) who can help you leverage technologies like AI and Blockchain to grow your business faster.

Companies in our program receive <YOUR INVESTMENT AMOUNT> in funding along with access to our large mentor network and investors.

Would this be of interest to you?

You can visit <YOUR WEBSITE> to learn more, or reply to this email with any questions you may have. Since I found your company you can 'skip the line' of applications and go right to an interview with our investment partners.

Please let me know soon if you would like to interview.

<YOUR NAME>
<YOUR TITLE>

Managing Interviews and Pipeline

Now the fun really begins. You get to start meeting the companies in your pipeline. As we've mentioned, a healthy pipeline may have to conduct around 200 interviews. That can be a daunting task for any team, especially a small and potentially brand new accelerator team. So, how do you survive such a guantlant? Here's my survival tips so don't end up living on a video meetings for the foreseeable future.

To start, all these interviews need to be incredibly short and to the point. We're talking 15 minutes. They need to be short and jam-packed with as many questions as possible. This is a challenge both for the founder and the interviewer. Let's face it, in startup land both parties like to talk a lot and often have to explain things in great detail. Unfortunately, there's just no time for that here and the 15-minute deadline helps to avoid either party ranting for too long.

If a founder asks to use a slide deck just tell them "No". The reason for this is that there's no time for long presentations, and founders often ramble when using slides. This means there will be little time at the end of the presentation for questions and answers, which is the real important part of an accelerator interview. In my experience, yes - you will get a lot of grumbling from founders over this. They use the slides as a crutch and as such can be too dependent on them. That's also a bad signal. Great founders can speak naturally about their company and enjoy answering your direct questions without hesitation or frantically gasping for air.

For efficiency's sake I recommend starting every interview saying this:

"Thanks for joining us. Today we just have 15 minutes to talk and we have a lot of questions. So please try to keep all answers short so we can get through them. To get us started please give us your quick elevator pitch in under one minute."

This helps to set the proper expectations with the founder and remind everyone of our time limitations. A great accelerator interview has a lot of back and forth discussion. It shouldn't be a recap of the startup's entire history. It's more important to know where they are today, what drives them and to find out if they are truly ready for acceleration.

I've included a set of sample interview questions below, but it's a good idea to create your own list and iterate upon them as you get more experienced with interviews. I would also recommend saving the last 2 or 3 minutes to give them a chance to ask you questions. After conducting well over a thousand of these interviews I've also figured out this is a good signal about the founders' intent and experience level.

Smart founders ask:

Tell me about your mentor network, do you have anyone who is a good match for us?

Do you offer any follow-on investment?

Can you share some examples of companies you've invested in, relevant to us?

Dumb founders ask:

Do you provide housing for us? (They haven't even got in yet and if they are worried about where to stay, it's a bad sign)

Are your investment terms negotiable? (Again, they are not in yet and think they can bargain? LOL)

No, I can't think of any. (Smart founders ask questions.)

> **SURVIVAL PRO TIP**
>
> For conducting quick and efficient video interviews I recommend using Whereby (https://whereby.com). There's no login and downloads for guests and it works in most major browsers. It really helps to avoid losing the first few minutes of any meeting when everyone is trying to login and fix their sound settings.

Sample Interview Questions

Tell us about the founders' backgrounds?

How big is the opportunity you're working on?

What do you know about this space that others don't?

How do you market your product/service today?

How do you make money?

What's your biggest challenge today?

What's your current burn rate?

Why do you want to do this business for the next 5-10 years?

Any questions for us?

Selection Process

Now, it's time to pick your companies. Hopefully, you've managed to build a large and diverse pipeline to choose from. A very healthy pipeline might have around 1000 companies but this might be significantly smaller for newer programs or programs that serve a very specific niche. Benchmark programs like 500 Startups received around 3000 applications each batch. Whereas Y Combinator can receive 7500 or more applications.

Regardless of the size of your pipeline, your next step is to determine the top 20% that will receive interviews. That means if your deal flow pipeline is around 1000 companies you might be doing some 200 interviews. That's a lot of interviews, so you want to properly qualify them before scheduling the time.

In a startup accelerator pipeline I would start with the following deal stages:

- Lead (Your outbound and scouted companies)
- Applied (Anyone who came through your application form)
  When it's time to start screening the companies down to interviews I would then use deal stages like the following:
- Not a match (To screen out companies you should not be spending any time on)
- Weak Candidate (For companies that are relevant to your program but you're just not super excited about the opportunity)
- Too early (A good match for your program but they are too early stage. Putting them here makes it easy to follow up with them for later batches)
- Strong Candidate (Super strong company you're just not ready to interview yet. Use this stage to get a second opinion, and do more research on the company or industry they operate in)
- To be interviewed (They are checking most of your boxes and in the top 20% of your application pool)

RUNNING YOUR PROGRAM

Onboarding

Just like when you market a startup's product, you can never onboard too much. This doesn't have to wait until your program kicks off. Before the founders arrive you should be collecting information from them and providing it as well. The more of this you can get out of the way ahead of time the less it'll bog you down during the program itself.

Information to request in advance:

- Investment-related and due-diligence requests
- Founder contact information and emergency contacts
- Dietary restrictions

- Team size attending program to help you space plan
- T-shirt and hoodie sizes for swag
- High-resolution startup logos to include on your website and other materials

Information to send in advance:

- Program calendar
- A general FAQ with questions that keep coming up
- Information about the local region for founders traveling in
- Housing recommendations
- List of your partner deals so they can start applying for them
- An awesome welcome email to make everyone feel excited and informed

It's also recommended that your program operations people reach out to each company and set up a meeting. This time can be used to discuss things such as arriving and accommodation or visa related questions from international founders. It's also a great opportunity to understand the founders' expectations for the program.

Day 1 Kick-Off

The first day of an accelerator program is a lot like the first day of school. A bunch of young (and sometimes not so young) founders flowing into your office space, Doe-eyed and ready to learn while meeting their batchmates and awkwardly figuring out where to sit. It's a good day in the program and everyone is feeling excited about what's to come. The staff has typically been running around frantically to set things up and are finally starting to see the fruits of their hard work. Make the first day a great day for everyone and allow plenty of time for them to settle, get to know each other and get acclimatized to the surroundings. There's no need to rush everyone into the program curriculum and start grinding away on this first day. Better to ensure everyone is happy and knows where to find things.

The first-day agenda may look something like this:

08:00 - 11:30	Arrivals and get settled at your desks
11:30 - 12:00	Program Introduction
12:00 - 1:00	Batch Group Lunch
1:00 - 4:00	Meet your POC (Point of Contact)

As you can see it's a very light day, program wise. If you have any founders who have flown in internationally, they'll greatly appreciate this as well! Make sure to have someone greet everyone who arrives, and help them get settled. Get everyone seated, on the WIFI and with some coffee or snacks as they settle in and meet the rest of the group.

At some point before lunch you should consider doing a quick program introduction. This is where the Program Director should gather everyone and officially kick-off the program! Emotions and some tensions are likely high at this point so use that to make it exciting. Everyone should feel like they're part of something great and have worked hard to get to this point. Don't worry about going into every detail of what the program is just yet. There will be time for that later. Instead, set some ground rules and introduce some of your processes. It's also good to do a round of introductions with each founder or company so that everyone starts to connect names and faces. That'll also help as you lead into a group lunch and batchmates have a little more to talk about. This can further be facilitated by doing some icebreaker sessions. Here are two ideas for that:

Drawing each other: Line up two rows of chairs facing each other. Ask the companies to sit next to their teammates as they'll be interacting with the person seated directly across from them. Give everyone a piece of paper, a pen, and something to lean on such as a clipboard. Once they are sitting there and ready, tell them, "Now draw the face of the person sitting across from you". This will typically result in some gasps and giggles. It's a fun exercise and a challenging one. For non-artists, this is actually very difficult! Although the point of the exercise is not to show off your artistic skills. Give them 5 minutes to complete the drawing and then ask them to take turns presenting their masterpieces to each other. This will generate some great discussions about each person and their background.

What's in the bag? Split your founders up into several groups, have them sit in a circle and ask them to bring their backpacks and/or purses. Go to each group and select one bag and then dump the contents of the bag into the center of the group. Then ask the group to go through the items and try to figure out whose bag it is and what type of person the owner is. The owner themselves must sit there quietly without revealing anything about themselves or the contents of the bag. Give them 5 minutes for this, then ask each group to present their findings.

For the remainder of the day, founders are still getting settled, although things might be a bit more hectic for the program team. Use the time to set up meetings where each company sits down for 45-60 minutes with their POC (point of contact). This is a chance for them to introduce themselves and field any immediate questions the founders have. It's also a great time for sharing with the founder how to best work with their POC.

Finally, you might be eager to set up a social night on the first day, but I don't recommend it. Save the first team social night for the first Friday of week one. On day one, everyone is likely to be a bit overwhelmed and those who have traveled in that day will be both tired and jet-lagged. Let everyone get out early and get to their housing and settle in.

**** SURVIVAL PRO TIP ****

I recommend having a small swag box waiting at everyone's desk. This can include things such as stickers from your program, t-shirts and hoodies, an information sheet, swag from partners and other things. It's a very small gesture but has a big impact on founders. As a program marketing bonus, and due to their excitement, they'll be eager to add your program's sticker to their laptop right away.

Typical Week

Before you start filling out your program calendar, it's recommended to first consider what a typical week looks like. For both your own sanity and to help the founders find a rhythm you'll want to have some predictability to each week. This includes what type of sessions are on which days and ideally these should be scheduled consistently throughout the program.

Monday	• Morning Standup and Batch Check-in
Tuesday	• Expert Talk/Workshop • Pitch Prep Session
Wednesday	• Get out of the office day
Thursday	• Mentor Office Hours
Friday	• KPI Review Session • Social Dinner

Program Curriculum Calendar

Having experimented with several different formats for program calendars and curriculum I've found that having thematic weeks is typically the best approach. This makes it easy to schedule the relevant mentors for that week and helps the founders mentally prepare for both the current week and the weeks to come. It also allows the founder to optimize their team's travel needs if the program takes place outside of their home country. For example, the founder can include marketing team members for the weeks where growth marketing is covered. For heavily technical weeks the CTO can take a larger role. When the content is not relevant for them they can then skip some of that time to address the day to day needs of the business.

In terms of program length, the most common structure is a 3-month program. Although it's possible to run programs on a shorter cycle, say 1 month, these shorter programs are typically less impactful as it's too short of a time to show any significant results. They are a good match for a 'pre-accelerator' program, but to really go deep you need at least the 3 months. Programs that are longer than 3 months run the risk of founder and staff fatigue and less engagement in the tail end of the program. Those longer programs are more of an incubator format.

Additionally, there are several weekly recurring sessions you should consider for your program. They include:

Pitching (group session): Every team should pitch to a group or staff member every single week. Crafting a good pitch takes a lot of time and the only way to get great is to do it hundreds of times during the program.

POC Check-in (private session): Each team should meet with the POC from the staff at least once a week just to update and ask questions. Here's where you help them address any blockers they're having in terms of growth, fundraising or staffing.

KPI Session (group session): Get each founder to present their weekly KPIs and/or growth successes every week. This is a chance to hold founders accountable and motivate them to focus on the most important things they can do in a program to grow their business faster.

Motivating Founders

One could write an entire book on motivating founders and in fact several actually already exist. Perhaps the best example is '*Trillion Dollar Coach: The Leadership Playbook of Silicon Valley's Bill Campbell*'. So I'll do my best to summarize how to specifically motivate founders in an accelerator program.

The most important method for motivation in these programs is accountability. This falls mainly on the founder but also the program director or in this case more specifically the POC (point of contact). For the founder, you motivate them by helping to guide their business, setting goals and challenging them to complete tasks. This is best done on a weekly iterative cycle, with small deliverables. The POC then meets with the founder weekly to discuss how their last week went and what they plan to do next week.

Naturally, founders will have a million excuses for why they didn't complete deliverables. As POC, it's your job to help knock down blockers and push them to complete. Y Combinator is known to be ruthless in this regard. Their POCs accept few excuses and really push the founders when they don't follow through on what they committed to. It's tough love but it's the only thing that works with early-stage founders.

A few examples of weekly tasks might be:

- Send (10) outbound sales emails offering a demo
- Onboard an intern to support you during the program
- Start building an investor pipeline

I also encourage you to end each week with a batch-wide group forum, where the founders present the results from the week. I normally position this as a weekly KPI review session. Learn more about these meetings and how to structure them below. This helps support accountability in the batch as each founder will know how to present their week's achievements in front of their peers. If they failed to focus on their KPI for the week that creates some shame within the batch. At the same time, the program manager should be using that moment to help them remove blockers and enable them to come back next week with more results. You'll also see these meetings prompt a lot of group feedback and general founders-helping-founders type vibes.

KPI Tracking and Growth

When you ask founders why they want to join an accelerator program they usually only give two answers. First is the access to mentors and investors, followed closely by the fact that they want help with growth. It's an area that most founders struggle with. Growth in a startup not only has the biggest impact on their business but also their likelihood of a successful fundraise . To that end, we start by helping the founder understand, track and measure their KPIs and finally run experiments to activate growth.

Easier said than done of course. Most early-stage startups don't know their KPIs. They have limited data sets and they're generally awful about tracking things. So we have to roll things back a bit and help them simplify in this regard. This is done by forcing them to pick and focus on one main KPI (key performance indicator). In startup-land, we also sometimes called this OMTM or *The One Metric that Matters*. This is great for use in an accelerator program because in a short program you don't have time to help them improve *all* their KPIs. Better to just focus on a key driver that impacts the business and/or will present well at the upcoming Demo Day.

I recommend having each company's POC (point of contact) establish this KPI during the first sit down meeting during the program. In some cases, founders will know which metric they want to pick and in others, you'll need to coach them on. During that meeting, or as part of the onboarding, provide them with a shared Google Sheet. You can download the template for this at http://accelerator.guide.

To start they enter their OMTM as specifically as possible. It should be highly measurable and preferably a metric that can be influenced during the program.

Examples of good accelerator OMTM:

- User signups
- MRR (Monthly recurring revenue)
- App downloads
- Outbound sales calls
- Orders placed

Examples of bad accelerator OMTM:

1. Enterprise sales contracts (takes too long)
2. Government contracts (takes even longer!)
3. Facebook fans (vanity metric)
4. Press hits (takes long and is unpredictable)
5. Amount of code shipped or new products launched (hard to measure)

Next, have them enter exactly what this metric is today. You may find in some cases founders don't even know the data point! If so, help them to locate and be able to measure this KPI more effectively. We also want them to predict what the metric will be at the end of the program. As a word of caution, it's actually very hard to effect any metric even in a 3-month long program. Things always take longer than you would expect and don't forget the founder will be busy with the other curriculum you have planned for them. So here's a chance for both POC and founder to be realistic in their forecasting.

Finally, we also give the founder the option to enter in some other goals. These should be more about qualitative goals and personal development. These goals also give the POC something to talk about during each sync meeting and for the founders to share with each other during the weekly group KPI review session.

Here's a version of the template:

Company name: <startup name>		
KPI	**Program Start**	**Program End**
<Insert metric name (OMTM)>	<add metric today>	<what you expect metric to be when the program ends>
Results		
Other Goals	<insert your qualitative goals>	
	<insert your qualitative goals>	

Once completed it might look something like this:

Company name: Sassy SaaS Thing Inc.		
KPI	**Program Start**	**Program End**
Weekly free user signups	100 Weekly Signups	200 Weekly Signups
Results		
Other Goals	Setup a better CRM	

Learn Google Adwords

The above examples are meant to be public, shared documents across all founders in the batch. This is both for easy management but also to encourage some transparency between batchmates. You shouldn't have any companies in a single batch who are competitive with each other. At the same time, these early-stage startups don't really have secrets valuable enough to not be shared with the group. At least not when it comes to their current metrics.

So as the weeks go on we use the same sheet, creating a column for each KPI sync meeting that occurs. During the meeting, this sheet is put up on a projector and each founder presents his or her tab separately. After each presentation, there's some time for the program staff to provide feedback. Be sure to also solicit the batchmates to contribute here as well. It's a great way to get some cross batch collaboration going.

Company name: Sassy SaaS Thing Inc.

KPI	Program Start	KPI Sync 1	KPI Sync 2	KPI Sync 3	KPI Sync 4	Program End
Weekly free user signups	100 Weekly Signups					200 Weekly Signups
Results		105	120	145	175	

Other Goals	Setup a better CRM	DONE		
	Learn Google Adwords	DONE		

RUNNING A VIRTUAL ACCELERATOR

If you would have asked me years ago if it's possible to run a high value accelerator program entirely online I would have told you absolutely not. The heart and sole of a good program is all about the experience of being together and the spontaneous opportunities to help founders that arise during the program itself. It's a bit of a fluffy thing to say but the best way to describe a good accelerator program is call it a serendipity engine for growth. And those serendipitous moments are tough to impossible to replicate online and over video meetings. So I generally did not believe that virtual programs were worth the effort both for program managers or the founders themselves.

Then COVID-19 happened.

The global pandemic has had a massive impact on accelerators around the world. Especially the leading programs located in Silicon Valley. After all one of the biggest values they could offer was bringing founders from around the world to the mecca of startups, even if just for a brief moment in time. For the time being that's not possible and even in the future I foresee that programs will adopt a hybrid form of in-person and online curriculum.

This is both good and bad for program managers and the startups. On the good side it makes programs more accessible as founders can attend them from anywhere in the world. No travel required which can be expensive and take them away from their teams. On the bad side it'll be more difficult to work with founders and keep them engaged. After a year of helping programs made the transition online let's review a few things I've learned.

Transitioning to Online

Thankfully the startup industry was well suited to make the 'pandemic shift' as our industry was already living and working online before it was trendy. We knew how online collaboration tools worked and were eager to leverage them more extensively in the work that we do. However that doesn't mean such a transition was an easy one to make.

Where I've seen most programs struggle with such a transition is when they try to replicate their entire in-person programs to a purely virtual format. While the online tools these days are robust they still, and I assume always will, fall short replacing the value of in-person teaching. And make no mistake, as a program manager you are a teacher and the startups are your students. You can perhaps take some solace in knowing your job is easier than say the grade school teachers who have had to manage a Zoom room of 25 young rambunctious children.

Keeping founders engaged

Let's be honest with ourselves and acknowledge that most online meetings are dreadfully boring. Now imagine you're a founder who has video meetings all day to run their business and now on top of that they have yet more video meetings, webinars and mentor sessions they must take part in for your program. Quickly they develop what has become known as 'Zoom fatigue' and it is down right exhausting.

Previously when leading programs and teaching sessions it was easy to tell who was engaged and who wasn't. You typically had a group of founders sitting right in front of you where it was possible to 'read the room' and gauge how well the content is resonating with them. That's significantly more difficult to do over video.

DEMO DAY SUCCESS

Demo day is the cherry on top of your hopefully successful accelerator program. It's a chance for startups to show off their progress (AKA recent acceleration) and connect with investors. For investors, it's a chance to connect with early-stage startups before they get too far along (aka too expensive). It's a very symbiotic thing and all Demo Days generally follow the same format more or less:

- Introduction to program
- Thanking of sponsors
- A series of 2-3 minute startup pitches
- Break
- The remaining 2-3 minute startup pitches
- Mixer and investor matchmaking

Some say that startup Demo Days are simply a dog and pony show. And let's face it they're not totally wrong. There is much pageantry and embellishment of hockey stick growth charts going on after all. Still, it's a tried and true format so I would recommend including one in your program.

You are of course welcome and encouraged to innovate or individualize your Demo Day in some way. This helps with audience engagement and future attendance as well. Even for the most seasoned investors, it's tough to sit through 10+ pitches back to back and not get a bit exhausted. So do what you can to keep them in mind in terms of event pacing and additional content.

As an example of a not so-great Demo Day that I once attended, there was over 1 hour of pre-programming and 'words from our sponsor' before we got into the many many startup pitches. This was a large program as well so the demos went on for several more hours! This, along with a lack of breaks, was more of a marathon than a pitch night. I even saw one poor investor leaning his head back and passing out before it was all over. Be sure to be respectful of attendee's time, especially the investor's time.

I've also personally tried to make Demo Days a much more fun and entertaining event. I am an American after all. This has included everything from creating original video content, having comedians on stage and an Oprah Winfrey like moment where we placed small gifts under every chair in the audience. I even went as far as to have a rock band play at the halfway point. Let me tell you, there's nothing better than blasting a bunch of suited up investors with face-melting guitar solos and lead singer backflips to keep them awake and engaged. To this day some of them still tell me it was the greatest Demo Day they ever attended.

So as you can see it's not just the startups doing some pageantry to pull off a great Demo Day! That all being said, as a program director your mission for Demo Day is simple. Get the startups as many leads as possible. That's all Demo Day is - a lead generation machine to help your startups secure funding. Try not to lose track of this as you'll have a lot of stakeholders involved in your event and at the end of the day, you serve the startups. Of course keeping program sponsors and everyone else happy as well. Good luck!

Working with investors

Now to the important part of Demo Day. Parting investors from their money!

First, it's important to understand and accept that investments are almost never committed to right on the spot at Demo Day. The one exception here being Y Combinator where investors practically shower the startups in offers and term sheets. For most other programs however that is not the case. Demo Day is more about lead generation both for the investors and founders themselves.

You can, however, do a few things to ease the process for both interested parties. Much of this work should be starting well before Demo Day takes place, during your program. Build a list of your key investors and start inviting them to meet the startups right away. It's helpful if they can see where the company was at the beginning of the program, to compare progress once Demo Day comes around. I've found that investors that participate during the program through mentorship and office hours are more likely to invest in batch companies. They also tend to make for better investors.

For programs, I've also created a small list of what I call 'friendly investors'. These are a few investors that may or may not invest in my accelerator companies. It's actually better if they're not going to invest, as they'll be even more honest. They often also have some close attachment to the program/fund or perhaps to the program director. It's well understood that they'll make time to hear pitches but also give *very* candid and honest feedback. Even when that feedback can sometimes be negative, or as we like to call it, 'tough love'. These types of investors are incredibly helpful to get in front of your startups before Demo Day, to iron out the kinks in their pitches. You can even tell the founders that these are your friendly investors, to help ease some of the stress they might be having over pitching.

As you get closer to Demo Day, start building your even larger investor list. Try to think of everyone you can who might be relevant. In some cases, this might also include corporate partners, press and local startup community leads. When it comes to investors themselves they are tricky to lock down into a date. After all, these are people who spend a lot of time traveling and in other pitch meetings. So you can't notify them soon enough of when your Demo Day is coming up. I recommend sending 'Save the Date' notifications and calendar invites at least 60 days before your event takes place. Don't be afraid to follow up several times to confirm attendance. After all, come Demo Day, if you don't have a good selection of investors in the audience your startups will be severely disappointed.

Some programs like to keep their list program companies secret to investors during the program. Perhaps this might be a way to encourage attendance at the Demo Day itself as it provides so-called exclusive access to the startups. I don't agree with this approach however, and as such recommend sending lots of materials, your startups' contact info and other assets well ahead of Demo Day. Investors like to read up beforehand and record the startup's information in their own CRM (Contact Relationship Management software). This I feel can help to increase the chance of investors approaching startups they like at the event. Even better, sometimes investors and founders will start emailing each other prior to Demo Day. That'll make their first meeting and following meetings just that much more efficient.

The day after Demo Day

When this day finally comes, both you and your startups are likely to be breathing a sigh of relief. You have both made it to the end of the program and it's time, as it were, for the little birdies to leave your safe nest and venture out into the big big world. Before they do however it's good to ensure they are maximizing their opportunities from Demo Day.

In startup investing there's a certain excitement after you first meet a startup you like. Since this often happens right after a Demo Day, it's your startups' best chance to capitalize on it. So it's recommended to have your founders not relax too much after Demo Day and instead strike while the iron is hot. That is to say, they should start reaching out to contacts made at Demo Day and book meetings as quickly as possible. With each passing day, there's a chance the investor will lose interest or worse, get distracted by yet another Demo Day. So you want to capitalize on their interest quickly.

Additionally, in many programs you have startups coming in from other parts of the world. That also means they are likely heading back home soon after the program wraps. So, in this case, they have limited time to get those investor meetings booked. They also have a slight advantage as the investors have limited time to book a meeting before they go. Have your startups use this in their outreach emails as so:

"It was great to meet at Demo Day last night! We are in town for just next week. Possible we could come by Monday or Tuesday to discuss further?"

Regardless of if the startups are local or not, you want to advise them to push for meetings quickly. As we have discussed, Demo Days are primarily a lead generator for your startups. Any salesperson will tell you the slower you close a lead the less likely it will close at all. So give them one last accelerator boost in this regard to get those meetings on the books and hopefully soon funding will be in the bank.

ALUMNI AND FOLLOW UP

Having personally conducted a few thousand accelerator screening interviews I can tell you that startups often ask:

"What do you offer in terms of alumni support after the program?"

It's a fair question after all, especially in the case where your accelerator program is taking equity from the companies. Founders want to ensure that you won't 'ghost' them after the program ends and that you'll continue to provide value. Some of the best programs in the world are very well known for the resources and network they provide to founders even years after they exit a program.

Regardless, and from my experience, once a program ends it's very much like high school. You don't ever hear from up to 75% of your accelerator ever companies again. That's because one of two things happen. Either the startup gets well-funded and scales like crazy, or they sputter out and die. In these two cases, they are either too busy to need alumni support or too out of business. In the former case, you'll have trouble just getting an email reply from them. And in the latter case, well, there's not much to talk about!

Programs that end up running many batches, however, will still build up a not-insignificant number of companies, founders, investments and other things to manage. Let's learn a few ways to approach this.

Program wrap up

First, before our little birds leave the nest, let's talk about how to close an accelerator program.

Measuring your program's success

Practice what you preach to the startups when it comes to gathering user feedback. As program managers, you should also be surveying each startup at the end of the program. It's recommended to use a very simple Net Promoter Score (NPS) as a minimum. Gathering your NPS score for each batch will allow you the easiest way to track your own performance. With each new batch, you can see if your program quality is improving or in decline. Spoiler alert - it should be getting slightly better each time.

What's an NPS Survey?

Even if you didn't previously know about NPS you have no doubt been presented with a survey yourself. Brands, especially large multinational and service-oriented businesses, often use this framework. It helps to quantify user sentiment and determine who will evangelize something in a format that most can agree upon. As you can imagine, word-of-mouth marketing and evangelism are very important for startup accelerator programs. So this format works well to measure your program in this regard.

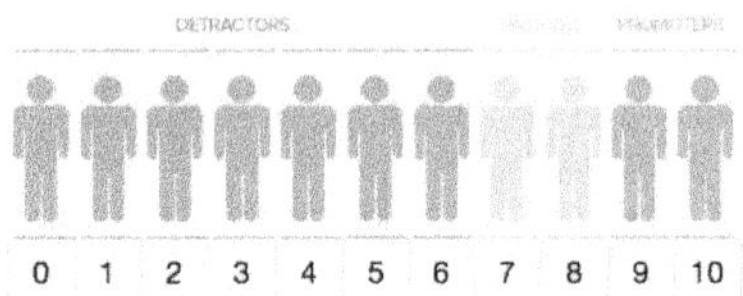

NPS focuses primarily on your biggest promoters. Disregard those who show low to medium interest in your brand.

You can also send a longer survey gathering additional information but as a warning, the more questions you put into a survey the lower the response rate. I've seen accelerators send surveys that looked more like complicated government applications. So use your own discretion and be mindful of the time-poor founder's time. An NPS survey and an open feedback field will probably be a sufficient amount of info to collect at the end of the program.

> **SURVIVAL PRO TIP**
> Send your founder surveys immediately after the program while the experience is fresh. Additionally, the longer you wait after Demo Day the less likely you are to get responses. Founders get busy again, or out of business before you know it.

Follow on Investing

During the interview process with startups, you'll inevitably get questions about follow-on investment. Yes, startups that haven't even got the first investment will typically already be asking about the next one. Such is the never-ending fundraising cycle many founders find themselves in. At the same time, it's a unique value add when a program can not only add some initial capital but also further funding should everything go well. It's also not such a bad deal for the startup program. After all, they'll be spending 1-3 months side-by-side with the startup and get a unique insight into how the founders operate. It's a level of due-diligence not even the most thorough and detailed venture firm would get a chance to conduct. So it's perhaps safe to assume you might be able to pick a few of the winners from the batch at large.

Conclusion

Well you've made it to the end of this book and hopefully to the end of your first program. Or perhaps you learned a thing or two to apply to your next batch. Having run many accelerators I wanted to leave you with something that's not so easy to quantify or share with you within these pages. That a successful accelerator program is able to capture a certain level of magic between the staff and founders. It's not something that can be taught by me or likely anyone else. It's something special and when you manage to create it you'll just know. You'll see it on the faces of the founders you work with. It'll come in the form of your founders' smiles and eternal gratitude both during the program and after. If they say things like, "this program was life changing", then you're on the right track.

This book, much like startups themselves, is not meant to be a static record or a definitive guide for how you must run your program. Take the learnings and make your program your own. Be sure to also visit https://accelerator.guide for additional resources, updates and supplemental content.

Glossary of Terms

Here is a list of common terms and acronyms used in startup accelerators and mentioned throughout this book.

Accelerator: A short curriculum-based program for startups typically taking place over 1-3 months.

Amazon Web Services (AWS): The cloud computing platform from Amazon who are actively involved in many startup accelerator programs.

Batch: A group of startups participating in startup accelerator programs. Sometimes also referred to as batchies.

Cohort: Same as a batch, it's a group of startups in a single program. Similar to a vintage of a wine.

Elevator Pitch: A quick startup pitch - given its name because it should be no longer than a ride in an elevator.

Entrepreneur in Residence (EIR): A serial founder who joins an accelerator or venture fund part-time while they work on their next startup idea.

Key Performance Indicator (KPI): An important metric within a startup used to track progress. For example, new user signups, monthly revenue and so on.

Incubator: Similar to an accelerator but taking place across a longer program time frame. Incubators also typically invest larger amounts of capital than an accelerator and take more company equity in exchange.

Mentor: An industry expert who meets with startups in an accelerator. This usually takes place in the form of group talks and individual office hour sessions.

Point of Contact: A designated member of the accelerator staff assigned to each company. It's who they meet with most often and where they start when they have a question.

Wantrepreneur: Low-quality founders without much experience who are trying to break into the startup scene. Often going about it all the wrong way, or doing it for selfish reasons.